Darrin Lunde

Illustrated by Patricia J. Wynne

Hello, Baby Beluga

ini Charlesbridge

Hello, swimming animal.
What is your name?

My name is Baby Beluga.

I am a kind of whale.

Baby Beluga, what do you look like?

I am five feet long.

My skin is dark gray.

It will turn white like my mother's
   when I am older.

Baby Beluga,
where do you live?

I live in the Arctic Ocean.

I like cold water.

Baby Beluga,
how do you live
in the cold water?

I have a layer of fat to keep me warm.

I breathe through a hole in the top

of my head.

Baby Beluga,
do you make any sounds?

I make many sounds.

I can chirp like a bird and moo like a cow.

I can make a loud whistling sound.

Baby Beluga, what do you eat?

I eat shrimp, squid, clams, crabs, and small fish.

I also drink milk from my mother.

Baby Beluga, what do you fear?

I am afraid of orca whales and polar bears.

They try to eat me.

Baby Beluga,
do you live alone?

I live with a large pod of other belugas.

I stay close to my mother

  and other belugas my age.

Baby Beluga, how do you sleep?

I float on the water.

I do not sleep deeply.

Good night, Baby Beluga!

Beluga babies are called calves.

They can swim as soon as they are born.

Adult beluga whales can grow to sixteen feet long.

They can hold their breath for more than ten minutes.

Beluga whales are very flexible.

They can turn their head from side to side.

They can swim backward and upside down.

Beluga whales sleep for eight hours each day.

They are never fully asleep, though.

Parts of their brain sleep while other parts stay awake.

For Midori—D. L.

For Captain R. E. Dooley, Jr.,
my last hero—P. J. W.

Published by Charlesbridge
85 Main Street
Watertown, MA 02472
(617) 926-0329
www.charlesbridge.com

Library of Congress Cataloging-in-Publication Data
Lunde, Darrin P.
   Hello, baby beluga / Darrin Lunde ; Illustrations by Patricia J. Wynne.
      p. cm.
   ISBN 978-1-57091-739-4 (reinforced for library use)
   ISBN 978-1-57091-740-0 (softcover)
1. White whale—Juvenile literature. I. Wynne, Patricia, ill. II. Title.
QL737.C433L86 2011
599.5'42139—dc22   2010007550

Printed in Singapore
(hc) 10 9 8 7 6 5 4 3 2 1
(sc) 10 9 8 7 6 5 4 3 2 1

Illustrations done in watercolor, ink, colored pencil, and pastels on Arches hot-press paper
Display type and text type set in Garamouche Bold from P22 Type Foundry and Billy from SparkyType
Color separations by Chroma Graphics, Singapore
Printed and bound September 2010 by Imago in Singapore
Production supervision by Brian G. Walker
Designed by Martha MacLeod Sikkema